Fact Finders®

INVENT IT

HARNESS IT

INVENT NEW WAYS TO HARNESS ENERGY AND NATURE

by Tammy Enz

Project Consultant
Daniel Enz, P.E. PhD
Assistant Professor, General Engineering
University of Wisconsin, Platteville

CAPSTONE PRESS
a capstone imprint

Fact Finders are published by Capstone Press,
1710 Roe Crest Drive, North Mankato, Minnesota 56003
www.capstonepub.com

Books published by Capstone Press are manufactured with paper
containing at least 10 percent post-consumer waste.

Library of Congress Cataloging-in-Publication Data
Enz, Tammy.
  Harness it : invent new ways to harness energy and nature / by Tammy Enz.
      p. cm.—(Fact finders. Invent it)
  Includes bibliographical references and index.
  Summary: "Explains the principles of inventing and provides photo-illustrated instructions for making
a variety of projects that harness energy"—Provided by publisher.
  ISBN 978-1-4296-7633-5 (library binding)
  ISBN 978-1-4296-7982-4 (paperback)
  1. Power resources—Experiments—Juvenile literature. 2. Force and energy—Experiments—Juvenile
literature. I. Title. II. Series.
  TJ163.23.E59 2012
  621.042—dc23   2011028737

Editorial Credits
Christopher L. Harbo, editor; Sarah Bennett, designer; Eric Gohl, photo researcher; Marcy Morin,
    scheduler; Sarah Schuette, photo stylist; Laura Manthe, production specialist

Photo Credits
Capstone Studio: Karon Dubke, all cover and interior project photos
Library of Congress: 23 (bottom)
Shutterstock: Mike Flippo, 12 (bottom), MilaLiu, 16 (bottom), Rozhkovs, 27 (bottom)

Design Elements
Shutterstock: alekup, liskus, Sylverarts, Tropinina Olga

Printed in the United States of America in Brainerd, Minnesota.

102011   006406BANGS12

CONTENTS

POWER PLAY

Engineers and inventors are always looking for ways to use nature. They harness heat, light, and other kinds of energy in ways that improve people's lives. You don't have to look too far to find proof. The toaster you use harnesses electricity and heat energy. Your solar-powered calculator uses the power of the sun. But you don't have to wait for someone else to build the next great invention. You too can harness light, electricity, and nature in amazing, inventive ways.

THE SIX STEPS OF INVENTING

Engineers and inventors follow a certain method when inventing. This method helps them build on their successes and learn from their failures. Inventors call the method's steps by different names, but the basics are always the same. Follow these six steps to see how inventing works:

THE SIX STEPS OF INVENTING

1 PROBLEM → 2 PRINCIPLE → 3 IDEAS → 4 PLAN → 5 CREATE → 6 IMPROVE

1 PROBLEM Inventors usually start with a problem. Ask yourself—What problem am I trying to solve?

2 PRINCIPLE Principles are basic rules or laws for how things work. Gravity is a principle that explains why a ball falls when you drop it. Friction is a principle that slows a ball down when you roll it across the floor. Ask yourself—What rules or laws apply to the problem I'm trying to solve?

3 IDEAS Write down some ideas that could help solve your problem. Be creative. Then pick the idea you think will work the best.

4 PLAN Plan how to build your device. Gather the tools and supplies needed.

5 CREATE Put everything together and make something new.

6 IMPROVE Once the solution is created, ask yourself if it solved the problem. If not, what can you change? If so, how can you make it better?

For each invention you build, the process starts all over again. Let's see these six steps in action with the inventions in this book.

PENNY BATTERY

1 PROBLEM It seems like every time you need to use a gadget, its battery is dead. Wouldn't it be great to create a power source from stuff you find around the house?

2 PRINCIPLE A battery uses a chemical reaction to make electricity. A reaction between different metals causes them to give and receive **electrons**. This flow of electrons is electricity.

3 IDEAS A battery can be made with two types of metals and an **electrolyte** that allows electrons to flow. You can try combinations of nickel and copper coins and tin or aluminum foil. Acids make good electrolytes. Lemon juice and vinegar are common acids.

4 PLAN

Gather together:
- ✔ 10 old copper pennies (dated before 1982)
- ✔ small dish
- ✔ vinegar
- ✔ toothbrush
- ✔ 12-inch (30-centimeter) square piece of aluminum foil
- ✔ pencil
- ✔ scissors
- ✔ paper towel
- ✔ tweezers
- ✔ plastic wrap
- ✔ voltmeter

electron—a tiny particle in an atom that travels around the nucleus
electrolyte—a substance that is capable of conducting an electric current when melted or dissolved in water

 CREATE

1 Place the pennies in a dish of vinegar. Scrub them with a toothbrush until they appear clean. Let them dry. Discard the vinegar.

2 Fold the foil in half four times until you have a small square. Trace a penny onto the foil. Cut the foil in the shape of a penny. Separate the pieces of foil into individual circles.

3 Repeat step 2 with the paper towel.

4 Fill the dish with more vinegar.

5 Place a penny on a flat surface. Using the tweezers, dip a paper towel circle into the vinegar for a few seconds. Carefully lay the paper towel circle on top of the penny. Make sure it completely covers the penny.

CONTINUED ON NEXT PAGE ➔

6 Use the tweezers to place a foil circle on top of the paper towel. Place a penny on top of the foil.

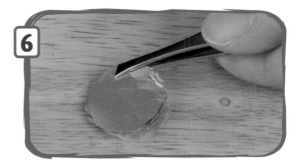

7 Repeat steps 5 and 6 until all the materials are stacked. A penny should be on the bottom and a foil circle should be on top.

8 Wrap the stack of pennies with plastic wrap to hold it together. Leave the top and bottom uncovered.

9 Carefully place one wire of the voltmeter under the bottom of the stack. Touch the foil circle on top of the stack with the other wire. The voltmeter should show that your battery is producing electricity.

6 IMPROVE

Did your battery have enough power to register on the voltmeter? Try connecting a small flashlight bulb or buzzer to the battery. If you need more power, make the penny stack taller. Or try making several of these batteries and connect them together.

SOLAR-POWERED MARSHMALLOW ROASTER

1 PROBLEM
You love s'mores, but you're not allowed to start a campfire in the backyard to make them. Can you invent a device that uses the sun to roast marshmallows?

2 PRINCIPLE
Solar power is energy from the sun. It can be very powerful. It can provide heat energy to cook food. But solar energy needs to be collected and focused.

3 IDEAS
A shiny curved surface can collect and focus sunlight. You can also collect and focus sunlight by using mirrors and lenses.

4 PLAN

Gather together:
- ✔ ruler
- ✔ pencil
- ✔ large cardboard oatmeal container
- ✔ utility knife
- ✔ black paint
- ✔ paintbrush
- ✔ medium-sized binder clip
- ✔ 3½-inch (9-cm) magnifying glass
- ✔ large rubber band
- ✔ large cardboard cereal box, flattened
- ✔ scissors
- ✔ aluminum foil
- ✔ masking tape
- ✔ 4-inch (10-cm) square mirror
- ✔ marshmallow
- ✔ wood skewer
- ✔ small wood wedges

CONTINUED ON NEXT PAGE ➡

9

 **CREATE**

1 Use a ruler and a pencil to measure and mark out a large rectangle on the oatmeal container. Starting at the bottom of the container, your rectangle should be 6 inches (15 cm) high and 4½ inches (11 cm) wide.

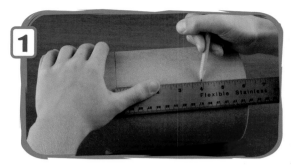

2 Have an adult cut the rectangle out of the container with a utility knife. Discard the rectangle.

3 Paint the inside and outside of the container black with a paintbrush. Let the container dry.

4 Attach the binder clip to the rim of the magnifying glass. The binder clip should be directly across from the magnifier's handle.

5 Fit the magnifier **horizontally** into the rectangular opening in the oatmeal container. Half of the magnifier will be inside the container and half will be outside. Wrap the rubber band around the magnifier's handle. Stretch the rubber band around the back of the container, and hook it to the binder clip.

horizontal—flat and parallel to the ground

6 Measure and mark out a **trapezoid** on the cereal box. The top of the trapezoid should be 10 inches (25 cm) long. The left and right sides should be 12 inches (30 cm) long. The bottom of the trapezoid should be 18 inches (46 cm) long. Cut out the trapezoid with a scissors.

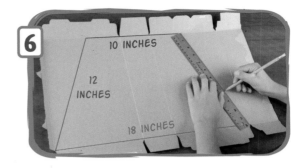

7 Use a ruler to measure in 6¾ inches (17 cm) from the bottom-right corner of the trapezoid. Mark this spot with a pencil. Draw a line from this mark to the top-right corner of the trapezoid. Fold the cardboard along this line.

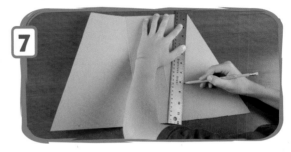

8 Repeat step 7 on the left side of the trapezoid.

9 Carefully wrap the cardboard in foil. Tape the foil in place. Try to keep the foil as wrinkle-free as possible.

10 Slide the trapezoid up to the opening in the container. Loosely tape the folded flaps to the sides of the opening. Leave some room to adjust the magnifying glass.

CONTINUED ON NEXT PAGE →

trapezoid—a shape with four sides of which only two are parallel

11 Slide the mirror beneath the magnifying glass.

12 Place the oven in a sunny place. Stick a marshmallow on the skewer. Lay the skewer across the top of the oatmeal container. Prop wedges under the mirror and twist the magnifier so you are able to focus sunlight on the marshmallow. As one area of the marshmallow melts, turn it to cook the other sides.

Were you able to roast your marshmallow? How long did it take? Can you cook anything else with the roaster?

➡ UNINTENDED SIDE EFFECTS

Dr. Percy Spencer was an engineer for the Raytheon Company in 1945. He was working with a magnetron to create radio signals. One day he noticed a candy bar in his pocket had melted. He wondered what had caused it to melt. He then tried putting popcorn in front of the magnetron. To his surprise, it popped! Spencer soon realized the microwaves from the magnetron could cook food. In 1947 he invented the first microwave oven.

NATURAL WATER FILTER

1 PROBLEM The rainwater that collects in mud puddles is filthy. Can you invent a way to make it clean again?

2 PRINCIPLE Look at how nature cleans water. Snow and rainwater seep through layers of rock, sand, and clay. This process filters out dirt and fills underground lakes and rivers with clear water.

3 IDEAS How can you imitate nature's process? Try using sand, gravel, and other materials to filter dirt and other particles out of water. Filter out larger particles first and smaller particles last.

4 PLAN

Gather together:
- ✔ empty 2-liter soda bottle
- ✔ scissors
- ✔ push top cap (to fit on 2-liter bottle)
- ✔ 12-inch (30-cm) long 2 x 4 board
- ✔ 8-inch (20-cm) long 2 x 4 board
- ✔ 2 3-inch (8-cm) long framing nails
- ✔ hammer
- ✔ 3 large rubber bands
- ✔ 6-inch (15-cm) square cotton cloth
- ✔ 4 cotton balls
- ✔ clean sand
- ✔ washed gravel
- ✔ 2 drinking glasses
- ✔ dirt
- ✔ water

CONTINUED ON NEXT PAGE →

 CREATE

1 Cut the bottom 3 inches (8 cm) off the soda bottle with a scissors.

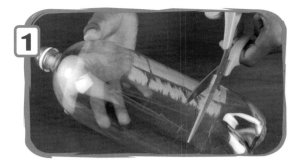

2 Screw the push top cap on the top of the bottle.

3 Stand the long 2 x 4 on end. Place the short 2 x 4 on top of it. Line up the edges of the boards to form an upside-down "L." With an adult's help, nail the two boards together with the hammer. Be sure to space the nails evenly.

4 Turn the "L" over. Place the soda bottle upside down against the inside of the "L". Strap the bottle to the wood with three rubber bands.

5 Place the cotton cloth inside the bottle across its neck. Make sure it rests smoothly against the sides of the bottle.

6 Place the cotton balls on the cloth and push them into the bottle's neck.

7 Fill the bottle about half full of clean sand. Make sure to keep the cloth flat to the sides of the bottle.

8 Fill the bottle almost full of gravel. Leave about 4 inches (10 cm) empty at the top.

9 Place a clean drinking glass under the bottle's tip.

10 Mix the dirt with some water in another glass. Pour it into the open end of the bottle.

CONTINUED ON NEXT PAGE ➜

11 Watch the clear water that trickles into the glass. While this filter will take out most of the dirt particles, it doesn't remove chemicals from the water. This water is not safe to drink.

6 IMPROVE

Did clear water trickle out of your filter? Can you make it work better? What other materials would work well as a filter? Can you find ways to remove chemicals from the water too?

➡ TRY, TRY, AND TRY SOME MORE

Thomas Edison is famous for inventing the lightbulb. Edison knew electricity could be harnessed to light up our homes. But he had a tough time finding the right material for a lightbulb filament. He tried more than 1,600 times to get it right. Edison tried coconut fiber, fishing line, and even hairs from a friend's beard. He wrote more than 40,000 pages of notes as he worked on the project.

HYDROPONIC GARDEN

1 PROBLEM Your mom's potted plant keeps getting knocked over. Soil gets ground into the carpet. Can you invent a way to grow plants without messy soil?

2 PRINCIPLE Soil gives plants **nutrients**, water, and a stable base for their roots. **Hydroponics** is a method of growing plants without soil.

3 IDEAS Think of some ways to give a plant nutrients, water, and a stable base without using soil. You can build a hydroponic garden out of many different materials. You'll need a container to hold the plant. Then experiment with rocks or marbles to hold the plant in place. Try different plant foods to give the plant the nutrients it needs.

4 PLAN

Gather together:
- ✔ scissors
- ✔ vining house plant
- ✔ drinking glass
- ✔ liquid plant fertilizer
- ✔ empty 2-liter soda bottle
- ✔ water
- ✔ 12-inch (30-cm) x 3 inch (8 cm) cotton cloth
- ✔ small rocks

nutrient—a substance needed by a living thing to stay healthy
hydroponics—the science of growing plants in a solution of water and chemicals rather than soil

CONTINUED ON NEXT PAGE →

CREATE

1 Use a scissors to cut a stem with several leaves from a vining house plant. Place the cutting into a glass of water. Add a few drops of liquid plant fertilizer. Wait about a week for roots to begin growing.

2 Cut off the top third of the soda bottle with the scissors.

3 Turn the bottle's top upside down. Place it into the bottom of the bottle.

4 Fill the bottom of the bottle with water up to the bottle neck.

5 Pour a small amount of liquid plant fertilizer in the water.

6 Twist the cotton cloth into a long thin coil. Insert the coil through the bottle neck and into the water. Leave half of the coil in the top of the bottle.

7 Place the roots of the plant into the bottle top. Make sure the roots touch the coil.

8 Fill the bottle top with rocks to support the plant.

9 Place your planter in a sunny spot. Keep the plant watered, and your plant will continue to grow without soil.

 IMPROVE

Does your planter keep your plant alive without soil? Try growing plants in different materials. Experiment with different types of plant foods. Will soda or milk work?

TRIP WIRE

1 PROBLEM
You think somebody is sneaking into your room and swiping your stuff. Can you build a device that will catch the thief in the act?

2 PRINCIPLE
An electric buzzer goes off when it is connected in an electric **circuit**. An electric circuit is complete when each buzzer wire touches one end of a battery.

3 IDEAS
But how can you get a thief to unknowingly complete a buzzer circuit? The key to this problem is to interrupt one of the wires. Then design a device that will allow the wires to reconnect when a thief enters. You can design something the thief will step on to squish the wires together. Or you can design a hidden obstacle that the thief will trip on, allowing the wires to connect.

circuit—the complete path of an electrical current

4 PLAN
Gather together:
- ✔ small electric buzzer
- ✔ 12-inch (30-cm) long 2 x 4 board
- ✔ hammer
- ✔ 4 small nails
- ✔ electrical tape
- ✔ D-size battery
- ✔ clothespin
- ✔ wire stripper
- ✔ 8-inch (20-cm) long coated electrical wire
- ✔ drill
- ✔ 1⁄16-inch (0.2-cm) drill bit
- ✔ wood craft stick
- ✔ fishing line

1 Place the buzzer about 2 inches (5 cm) from one end of the 2 x 4. With an adult's help, hammer the nails to secure the buzzer to the board.

2 Tape the open end of the buzzer's black wire to the negative (-) end of the battery.

3 Take one half of the clothespin out of its spring. Wrap the open end of the buzzer's red wire around the clothespin half with the spring. The wire should be wrapped about ¼ inch (0.6 cm) from the clothespin's tip.

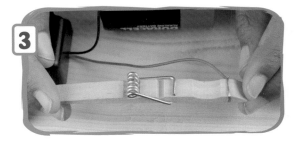

4 Place the clothespin half in front of the buzzer so it points toward the end of the 2 x 4. Pound one nail into the arched portion of the clothespin. Hammer the second nail about ½ inch (1.3 cm) from the other end of the clothespin.

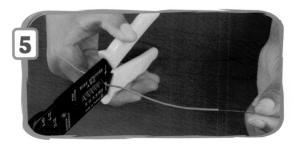

5 Use the wire stripper to remove about 2 inches (5 cm) of plastic coating from the ends of the 8-inch (20-cm) wire.

CONTINUED ON NEXT PAGE ➡

6 Wrap one end of this wire around the other clothespin half. The wire should be wrapped about ¼ inch (0.6 cm) from the clothespin's tip

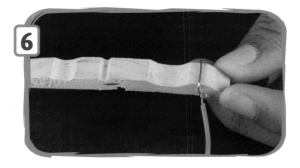

7 Put the clothespin back together. The wires wrapped around each half should touch.

8 Ask an adult to drill a small hole about ½ inch (1.3 cm) from one end of the craft stick.

9 Open the clothespin and insert the other end of the craft stick between the clothespin tips.

10 Tape the loose end of the 8-inch (20-cm) wire to the positive (+) end of the battery.

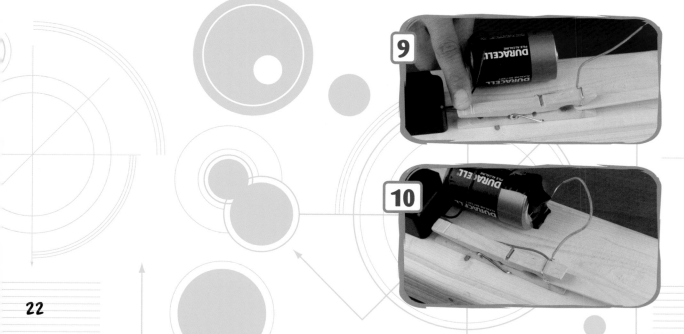

11 Tie fishing line through the hole in the craft stick.

12 Carefully stretch a length of fishing wire across a hallway or doorway. Tie the other end to a piece of furniture or other heavy object.

13 Wait for someone to walk by and snag the line with his or her foot. The craft stick should pop out of the clothespin. When the wires touch, the circuit is complete, and the buzzer goes off!

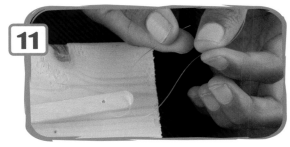

Did your trip wire work? Can you change this device so that it buzzes and lights up when someone trips it?

➡ EVER-CHANGING INVENTIONS

Harnessing fossil fuels to power the internal combustion engine was one of the greatest inventions of the last 200 years. In 1885 Karl Benz, a German mechanical engineer, designed and built the first practical automobile using this engine. The automobile was not like those we drive today. It looked more like a tricycle. The first patented gas-powered car had only three wheels!

23

WIND TURBINE

1 PROBLEM The wind is constantly blowing through your bedroom window. Can you build a device that harnesses wind power to make electricity?

2 PRINCIPLE A wind **turbine** turns wind power into electricity. Wind turns blades that cause a magnet to spin inside a **generator**. The spinning magnet produces electricity.

3 IDEAS How can you show this wind power in action? You'll need to build blades attached to a shaft. Plastic or cardboard would work for blades. You will then need something to act as a generator. Finally you'll need a way to detect that your turbine is producing electricity. A simple electromagnet, a tiny lightbulb, or a voltmeter can do this.

Gather together:
- ✔ pencil
- ✔ empty plastic gallon milk jug
- ✔ scissors
- ✔ 4 paper clips
- ✔ wire snips
- ✔ utility knife
- ✔ cork
- ✔ craft glue
- ✔ small plastic gear
- ✔ 1.5 volt DC motor
- ✔ electrical tape
- ✔ wooden ruler
- ✔ 2 6-inch (15-cm) lengths of coated electrical wire
- ✔ wire stripper
- ✔ 2 alligator clips
- ✔ voltmeter
- ✔ hair dryer

turbine—an engine powered by steam or gas

generator— a machine that produces electricity by turning a magnet inside a coil of wire

1 Draw four turbine blades on the flat surfaces of the milk jug. Make the blades 5 inches (13 cm) long. Make them ¾ inch (2 cm) wide at one end and 1½ inches (4 cm) wide at the other end. Cut out each turbine blade with a scissors.

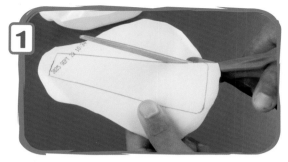

2 Bend the outer leg of each of the paper clips straight. Use the wire snips to snip each leg so it extends only 1 inch (2.5 cm) past the end of the clip.

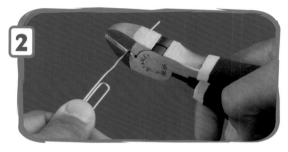

3 Have an adult use the utility knife to cut the cork in half. Throw away one half. Stick the end of each paper clip into the side of the remaining cork half. Each clip should sink about ½ inch (1.3 cm) into the cork. Make sure the clips are spaced evenly and at the same level around the cork.

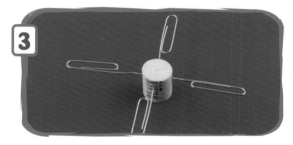

4 Slide the narrow end of one blade into one of the paper clips. Glue it in place. Repeat this step with the other three blades.

5 Glue the plastic gear to one end of the cork.

CONTINUED ON NEXT PAGE ➡

6 When the glue dries, slide the gear onto the motor shaft.

7 Tape the motor to one end of the ruler. Let the turbine blades hang off the end of the ruler.

8 Remove about 1 inch (2.5 cm) of plastic coating from the ends of the wires with the wire stripper.

9 Twist one wire around each of the motor terminals.

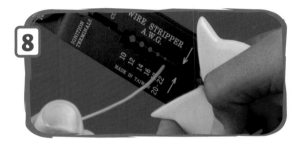

10 Connect alligator clips to the loose ends of the wires.

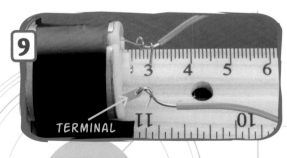

TERMINAL

11 Clip the alligator clips to the terminals of the voltmeter.

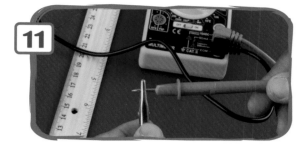

12 Twist each blade so that it is at a 45-degree angle from the motor shaft.

Did your wind turbine work? This design should produce up to 0.5 volts of power. Experiment with the angles and the sizes of the blades. Try to get more volts from the system. See if you can use it to light a tiny lightbulb.

13 Turn on the hair dryer and aim it at the turbine blades. As the blades spin, watch the reading on the voltmeter.

➡ BACKYARD INVENTING

Backyard tinkering can take you far. In 1888 Charles F. Brush built a backyard wind turbine. His invention contained 40 tons (36 metric tons) of iron and had 144 blades. It powered more than 350 lamps and three electric motors, fully powering his mansion. Brush's backyard tinkering led him to form the Brush Electric Company. His company later merged with other companies to form General Electric, a company that lights millions of homes today.

HIDDEN MESSAGE

1 PROBLEM You need to send a message to your best friend. But you don't want anyone else to read it. Can you create a way to write an invisible message?

2 PRINCIPLE An invisible ink needs to somehow become visible so a person can see it. Some **organic** substances dry clear but burn when heated. The organic material darkens when it burns, revealing the hidden message.

3 IDEAS Lemon juice, milk, and egg whites are clear organic liquids. Try one to see if you can make an invisible ink.

4 PLAN Gather together:
✔ paintbrush
✔ small dish of milk
✔ paper
✔ pencil
✔ oven
✔ baking sheet
✔ oven mitts

organic—part of an animal or plant

28

5 CREATE

1 Dip a paintbrush into a small dish of milk. Write a secret message on a blank piece of paper. Let the message dry.

2 Write a second message on top of the hidden message with a pencil.

3 Preheat the oven to 325 degrees Fahrenheit (163 degrees Celsius). Place the paper on a baking sheet. Then place the baking sheet into the oven for three to five minutes.

4 With an adult's help, use oven mitts to remove the baking sheet from the oven.

5 Read the hidden message that appeared.

6 IMPROVE

Did the message appear? Try different "inks" for writing your messages. Then try out different methods for revealing the message. Will a hair dryer, steam, or a microwave oven work to reveal your hidden message?

GLOSSARY

circuit (SUHR-kuht)—the complete path of an electrical current

electrolyte (i-LEK-truh-lite)—a substance that is capable of conducting an electric current when melted or dissolved in water

electron (i-LEK-tron)—a tiny particle in an atom that travels around the nucleus

filament (FI-luh-muhnt)—a thin wire that is heated electrically to produce light

generator (JEN-uh-ray-tur)—a machine that produces electricity by turning a magnet inside a coil of wire

horizontal (hor-uh-ZON-tuhl)—flat and parallel to the ground

hydroponics (hye-druh-PON-iks)—the science of growing plants in a solution of water and chemicals rather than soil

nutrient (NOO-tree-uhnt)—a substance needed by a living thing to stay healthy

organic (or-GAN-ik)—part of an animal or plant

patent (PAT-uhnt)—a legal document giving the inventor of some item sole rights to make or sell the item

trapezoid (TRAP-uh-zoid)—a shape with four sides of which only two are parallel

turbine (TUR-bine)—an engine powered by steam or gas

volt (VOHLT)—a unit for measuring electricity

READ MORE

Cook, Trevor. *Experiments with Electricity and Magnetism*. Science Lab. New York: PowerKids Press, 2009.

Taylor-Butler, Christine. *Super Cool Science Experiments: Solar Energy*. Science Explorer. Ann Arbor, Mich.: Cherry Lake Pub., 2010.

VanCleave, Janice. *Janice VanCleave's Super Science Challenges: Hands-On Inquiry Projects for Schools, Science Fairs, or Just Plain Fun!* San Francisco: Jossey-Bass, 2008.

INTERNET SITES

FactHound offers a safe, fun way to find Internet sites related to this book. All of the sites on FactHound have been researched by our staff.

Here's all you do:

Visit *www.facthound.com*

Type in this code: 9781429676335

Check out projects, games and lots more at
www.capstonekids.com

ABOUT THE AUTHOR

Tammy Enz became a civil engineer because of her awe of the massive steel bridges that spanned the Mississippi River. She just had to figure out how they worked. Today, she still likes tinkering and figuring out how things work. When she isn't tinkering, she fixes up old houses and conducts experiments in her garden and kitchen. Most of all, she loves reading books about anything and everything and asking "why?"

7-12